TABLE OF CONTENTS

LIST OF ILLUSTRATIONS

THE AMAZON PRIORITY FOR BRAZILIAN NATIONAL DEFENSE POLICY

The Brazilian Amazon includes eight states of the Federation, occupies an area of 5.2 million square kilometers, and is roughly equivalent to 61 % of the national territory. It contains a demographic density of 3.2 inhabitants per square kilometer, areas of tropical forests equivalent to one-third of the total existent on the planet, as well as the largest fresh water basin in the world. It also contains luxurious fauna and flora. Its wealth is practically untouched; studies indicate that it shelters the most varied and extraordinary mineral deposits on the globe. The extensive and largely uninhabited border regions have increasingly shown their vulnerability to penetration by individuals as well as organized narco-guerrillas and criminal elements.

The history of the development process in the Amazon has been featured by irregular efforts to integrate the Amazon into the rest of the national territory. During the previous administration, the Brazilian Government paid particular attention towards promoting economic and social development among the population in conjunction with environmental protection. This policy met with some success.

It is noted that the mission of defending the area had been the exclusive responsibility of the Armed Forces. In 1996, President Fernando Henrique Cardoso issued the first Brazilian National Defense Policy (BNDP). In this document, responsibility for defending the nation was assigned to society as a whole. Due to this new focus, governmental structure was changed - new ministries created, others disestablished, projects and responsibilities redirected to integrate matters related to national security. Among the most significant changes were the creation of the Ministry of Defense in July of 1999 and the abolishment of four military ministries - Army, Navy, Air Force and the General Staff of the Armed Forces.

In this context, this project seeks to identify, describe and discuss the actions that should be considered and implemented to establish one national strategy for Brazil's Amazon defense. In order to accomplish this purpose it first makes a short analysis of the BNDP through two levels: the international system and the nation-state. In turn, it describes the ways, means and ends that were established by this policy. Afterwards, it presents the geographic characteristics of the Amazon region, its problems and its main threats. Finally, the project shows the governmental actions that are taking place to implement Defense Policy in the Amazon region.

THE BRAZILIAN NATIONAL DEFENSE POLICY

The Brazilian National Defense Policy is designed to counter threats from achieving their objectives. It has, as its main purpose, the establishment of objectives for the defense of the nation at every level and in every sphere of power. In order to understand the determinant aspects that were considered to implement the ways, means and ends for the policy, this paper analyzes international influences and Brazilian state and national leadership, particularly that of the president

With the end of East-West confrontation and the current process of rearrangement of forces, an uncertain and unstable multipolar international environment has emerged. This has largely been the result of the lack of cooperation among the various centers of strategic, military, political and economic power; the future evolution of this unstable situation remains difficult to predict. During this transitional phase new rules of political and economic coexistence between nations are being established, characterized by the absence of clear paradigms as well as by the growing inclusion of non-governmental participants.

South America, thanks to its position, is far from the focal points of global tensions. During the Cold War, for example, U. S. defense policy toward Latin America was oriented towards keeping the region in a neutral security environment.[1] Even today, the U.S. Department of Defense (DOD) considers the region as an economy of force area.

The democratization as well as the integration processes that have taken place in the Americas have tended to reduce the likelihood of conflict in the hemisphere. Moreover, the region's history has amply demonstrated that nations have resolved regional disputes by using the mechanism of mediation, thus strengthening mutual confidence. In short, the concept of Latin America as a geopolitical secure area is still valid as long as there is no overall threat or intense world conflict.[2]

Throughout the 500 years of its history, Brazil has participated in few conflicts. During the twentieth century the nation has participated only in World War II. Brazil has no outstanding border disputes - by 1920, all disputes had been peacefully settled through diplomatic negotiation or international arbitration without ever resorting to the use of force. These facts contributed to the establishment of a National Defense Policy oriented towards pacific values. However, in spite of a favorable international situation, the actions of armed groups that are active in neighboring countries on the edge of the Brazilian Amazon, as well as international organized crime, are among the points that cause concern. These illegal activities can and do threaten Brazilian national interests.

Concerning the political situation in Brazil, the country is going through a phase of legal restructuring required by the new constitution. In 1988, Brazil's eighth constitution was introduced. It establishes the fundamental objects of the nation; principles for international relations; assigns missions for the Armed Forces, as well as declares that Brazil is a legal democracy founded on sovereignty, citizenship, the dignity of the human person, the social values of labor and of free enterprise and political pluralism.

Another important aspect is that Brazil is a country of different regions with a diversified profile - belonging simultaneously to the Amazon, Atlantic, Southern Cone and the Plata River Basin. The country has about 16,000 kilometers of land boundaries with ten different countries.[3] It also has a Continental Platform plus an Economic Exclusion Zone of about 4,5 millions square kilometers in the South Atlantic.[4] It features the Brazilian profile as simultaneously continental and marine, equatorial, tropical and subtropical. It generates a complex problem in planning a defense for the country which, of course, was considered in establishing the general plan.

From a close examination of the circumstances described above, we come to the conclusion that despite the favorable state of affairs in Brazil's immediate environs, the country is not totally free from risks. Therefore, a defense system, which is adequate to safeguard the nation's sovereignty, democracy

2

and the rule of law was created. This system is embodied by the National Defense Policy, which is built around an active diplomacy (devoted to peace) as well as a deterrent strategic posture, defensive in nature, based on the following principles:[5]

a. Borders and boundaries that are precisely defined and internationally recognized;

b. Close relationships, based on mutual respect and trust, with neighboring countries and with the international community in general;

c. Rejection of wars of conquest; and

d. Peaceful resolution of disputes, with resort to the use of force only for self- defense.

The National Defense Policy is concerned with the total involvement of the military and the civilian sector. In other words, it may include the strategic aims of the country in the social, economic, military and diplomatic spheres, and can count on the complete support of the nation. Therefore, the national defense objectives are:[6]

a. To guarantee sovereignty while preserving the Nation's territorial integrity, heritage and interests;

b. To guarantee the rule of law and democratic institutions;

c. To maintain the Nation's cohesion and unity;

d. To protect individuals, goods and resources that are Brazilian, or under Brazilian jurisdiction and to achieve or maintain Brazilian interests abroad;

e. To give Brazil a significant role in international affairs and a greater role in the international decision-making process; and

f. To contribute to the maintenance of international peace and security.

Finally, to establish a more concrete platform for implementing the objectives of national defense policy, the document presents guidelines that range from active participation in constructing an international order that can provide peace and sustainable development, to defense of the most vulnerable areas of the country such as the Amazon Region.

In such a manner, we can notice in the foregoing the natural multi-sectional policy and conception of national defense that seeks to involve the military and civil segments of government, the state and society as a whole in defense affairs.

In summary, Brazil is striving to establish its strategic role and its priorities in the area of defense free from any ideological model. Then, because of the national situation, the government has attributed a high priority to the Amazon Region

THE AMAZON REGION

GEOGRAPHIC ASPECTS

The Amazon, located in the northern part of South America, encompasses a total area of more than 6.5 million square kilometers, and is segmented among nine countries: Brazil, Venezuela, Colombia, Peru, Bolivia, Ecuador, Suriname, Guyana, and French Guyana. About 85 percent of this region is in Brazilian territory.[7]

3

In Brazil, the Amazon consists of two different concepts: The Geographic Amazon and the Legal Amazon. The Geographic Amazon includes the states of Amazonas, Pará, Rondônia, Acre, Roraima, Tocantins and Amapá. It represents an area of 3.5 million square kilometers, which corresponds to 42 percent of the entire national territory.[8] The region named the Legal Amazon, in Brazilian administrative terms, is composed of the following states: Acre, Amapá, Amazonas, Pará, Rondônia, Tocantins and Roraima as well as parts of the states of Mato Grosso, and Maranhão.

FIGURE 1 - GEOGRAPHIC AMAZON

The focus of this project is the Legal Amazon, hereafter simply called the Amazon. It occupies 5.2 million square kilometers, approximately 61 percent of the total area of the country. Its 16.5 million inhabitants equal about 12 percent of Brazil's total population. The demographic density of 3.2 inhabitants per square kilometer shows the area as a huge empty demographic entity.[9] Moreover, the population is concentrated in just a few urban nuclei and is distributed along the Amazon River and its main affluents.

The Amazon is a rich hydrographic basin, represented mainly by the Amazon River and its tributaries. It is responsible for approximately 20 percent of the global river flow into the world's oceans. The Amazon River discharge into the Atlantic, in one day, is almost the same water volume as the Thames River (England) in one year; the Mississippi River (United States) in twelve days; or the Congo River (Africa) in five days.[10] The rivers that exist in the Amazon basin have different cycles of flood and emptiness. Thanks to this fact, the Amazon River is navigable for about 23,000 kilometers.[11] Thus, fluvial navigation complements the poor road

FIGURE 2 - LEGAL AMAZON

networks in the region. The rivers are natural access routes for troop transport and logistic support. On the other hand, they are obstacles to military operations due to their width, depth and flooding propensities. Only a small portion of the Amazon can be described as a plain. Above the junction with the Rio Negro and the Rio Madeira, the plain widens out like a spatula, until a distance of some 800 miles separates the highlands to the north and those to the south. Non-solid gravel, sand, clay and silt underlie most of the surface of this large area. About 90 percent are above the level of the highest floods, because the flood plain of the main stream is usually less than 50 miles wide. Sharp bluffs stand 150 to 200 feet above the swamp along the river border of the flood plain. As the main stream meanders across the lowland, its channel shifts frequently, leaving oxbow lakes and swamps. Although forests of the rainy tropics are exuberant, the soil itself tends to be poor. Only on the river flood plains are there any substantial areas of fertile soil.[12]

Temperatures in the Amazon are high, but not excessive. In reality, they are lower than those that occur in summer in the Mississippi valley. At Manaus, for example, the highest temperature ever recorded is 101.5 $^{\circ}$F, and the lowest was 69.4 $^{\circ}$F. The highest temperature ever recorded in New York was 106 $^{\circ}$F.[13] Humidity, however, can be high enough in some areas to create discomfort. Rainfall throughout the North is abundant, even in the drier part of the year.

This combination of high temperature, humidity, rainfall, poor soil, exuberant forests and extensive flood plains make the Amazon hostile to human life. Moreover, its social and economic infrastructure is precarious. The main economic activities in the Amazon are mineral mining and vegetable extraction. Fishing is a fundamental activity needed to feed the riverine population. The Amazon is characterized as a raw material exporter. Only Manaus and Belem-Barcarena regions have an industrial district. Due to its poor infrastructure, Amazon living standards are below the national average. By and large, the population is poor and presents a low life expectancy with a high rate of infant mortality. In addition, there is a large incidence of typical endemic diseases such as malaria and social diseases such as tuberculosis due to inadequate sanitary conditions and medical insufficiency.

Geographical issues are not the Amazon's only problems. There are also agrarian, environmental protection, Indian lands, illegal mining, international interests and drug traffick.

THE AGRARIAN ISSUE.

At the beginning of 1980, during a period of military rule, the Landless Workers Movement (Movimento dos Trabalhadores Sem Terra - MST) started in the state of Rio Grande do Sul and resulted in a coordinated effort to occupy idle lands. These incursions by rural workers who called themselves landless multiplied and spread to other states. In the last few years, one region has become renowned because of its potential for violent conflicts, the state of Pará in northern Brazil - an area twice the size of France and with 80 percent of its territory covered by the Amazon rain forest.[14]

In Pará, the property situation is chaotic. There are immense unused and undocumented farms, widespread land usurpation (including Indian lands) and numerous prospectors and clandestine woodcutters (principally of mahogany). There have been no adequate alternatives for resettling families displaced by large farming projects and by the construction of hydroelectric dams like Tucuruí. These past mistakes have transformed part of Pará into a permanent area of conflict.

Historically, the south of Pará is an explosive area. At the beginning of the 1970's, the Brazilian Army was employed against the communist Araguaia Guerrilla Force near the city of Marabá.[15] In 1996, in Eldorado Carajás, the MST blocked an important road and confronted the police. As a result, several casualties occurred and a state of unrest ensued.[16]

There are several focuses of conflict in the Amazon region. They involve different actors. In Roraima, it is Indians against farmers; in Acré, rubber farmers, Indians, and agricultural farmers; in Rondônia, and Pará, farmers and squatters (posseiros).

INDIGENOUS ISSUES.

There are 554 indigenous lands in Brazil. The Brazilian indigenous people, who today number close to 330,000, occupy 11 percent of the national territory. About 60 percent of the Brazilian Indian population live in the Amazon region.[18]

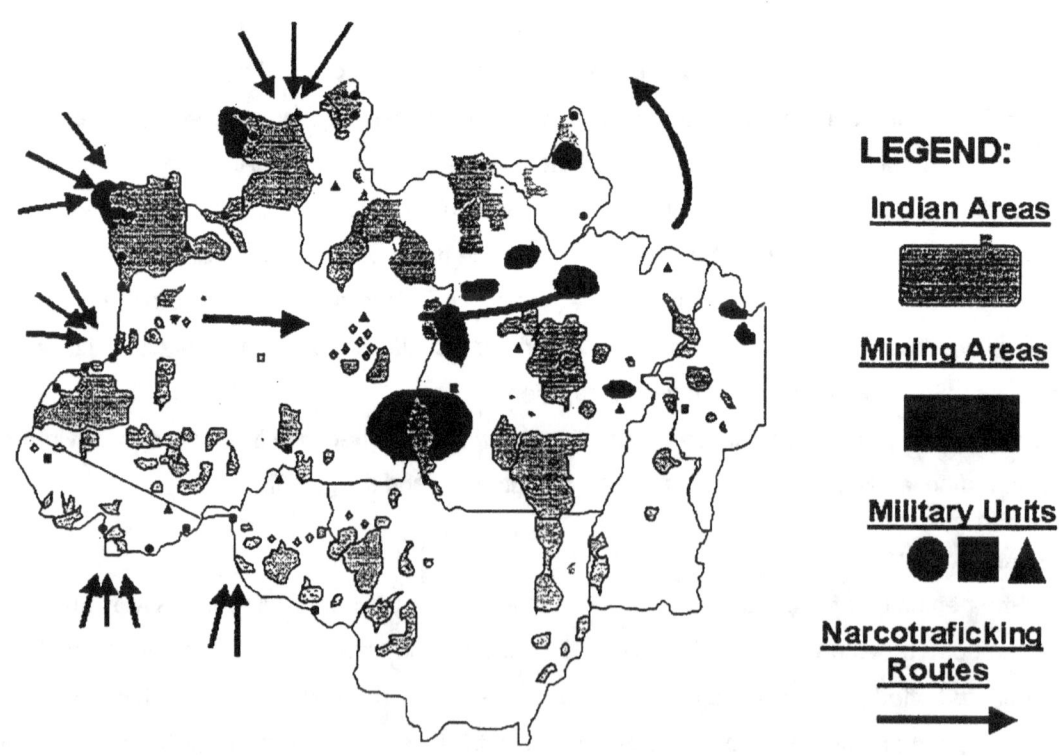

LEGEND:

Indian Areas

Mining Areas

Military Units

Narcotraficking Routes

FIGURE 3 - AMAZON ISSUES[17]

The Brazilian Government is implementing an indigenous policy that recognizes all of the rights of the Indians as set forth in the Constitution. On the other hand, the contact between the indigenous community and the civilized world has provoked conflict and has put Brazil in the uncomfortable position of having to face an adverse world public opinion. Thanks to this situation, Brazil was pressed by the international community to form "indigenous nations". The reality is that erroneous data published through the media about the Brazilian Indian problems resulted in adverse public opinion - formulated on this mistaken information the defense of any "indigenous nation" theory is much more problematic than just the economic damage created by this idea. For instance, in November of 1991 the Brazilian Government, under pressure, created the Yanomami Territory (an area equivalent to the size of Portugal) adjacent to the border with Venezuela. In the future, this will be able to create serious problems for the nation's territorial integrity.

Most of the Indian lands are located in areas difficult to access, close to national borders. Farmers, gold miners and adventurers also populate several of them. Other serious incursions include various "preservation" groups, missionaries, and religious activists among others. Some of these group activities have been directly contrary to their stated missions. Coincidentally, foreign evangelical missions are installed in areas potentially rich in precious or otherwise strategically valuable minerals.

The Indian issue is extremely complex. The Yanomami and other tribes in the areas have existing land rights that conflict with the claims of other groups. This pits the Indians against farmers, gold miners and woodcutters in frequent clashes, and requires a government presence to preserve order amidst the chaos thus generated.

THE ENVIRONMENTAL ISSUE.

The Amazon environmental issue was largely contested in Brazil and abroad. During the 1980's the international community became increasingly concerned about the destruction of Brazilian rain forests. Individuals and organizations in Brazil and around the world called for measures to slow or stop the destruction, although some complaints of non-governmental organizations are suspicious. Brazil views its rain forests both as a natural resource to be protected for mankind and as a source of wealth for its regional population and the country as a whole. Therefore, the great challenge to Brazil in the Amazon is to find a balance between the social-economic developmental process and human and environmental needs.

In this context, to effectively protect the environment, rationalize the use of natural resources and promote sustainable development in the Amazon, the government is thoroughly studying the potentialities and limitations of the region. In addition, it is implementing effective measures against the activities considered harmful to the national interest, such as predatory exploitation, drug traffic, and damage to the ecosystem and the occupation of the Indian reserves by non-Indian entities.

On the other hand, the country is very concerned about some threats hidden behind the environmental protection issue. For example, individuals and groups such as "People of the Forest," rubber gatherers or "tappers," nut gatherers, fishermen, lumber interests, small farmers and indigenous people, all who depend on the forest for their livelihood cause some serious problem. Brazil has received international pressure regarding these groups. It can be imagined, in the future, Indians and rubber tappers, supported by foreign countries, will be able to claim autonomy and self-government inside the Amazon.

THE DRUG ISSUE.

Colombia, Peru and Bolivia are the largest cocaine and other drug producers while the more developed countries contain the most consumers. The American government 's concern with increased drug consumption among its populace has focused its major strategy towards combating drug traffic by reducing the cultivation of drug producing crops and interdicting the flow of drugs at the source and in transit.

The escalation of the drug war in the Andean region has led narco-traffickers to change their shipment routes, and Brazil is increasingly being used as a route of choice. In addition, some drug producers have used Brazil as a shelter from the security forces in their own countries. These developments pose a direct threat to Brazil's national sovereignty.[19]

In Colombia, for instance, the Revolutionary Army Forces of Colombia (FARC) have become allies of the narco-traffickers. On 26 February 1991, a FARC unit of about 40 men attacked a Brazilian Army detachment that was stationed in a semi-permanent camp on the bank of the Traíra River on the border between Brazil and Colombia. The Brazilian unit of 17 men suffered casualties of 3 dead and 12 wounded. The guerrillas escaped carrying radio equipment, ammunition, uniform and all weapons at the camp.[20]

In a later combined operation with the Colombian Army, it was proven that the FARC guerrillas were allied with Colombian cocaine dealers and illegal miners. With the assistance of some Indians corrupted by the narco-guerillas, they had attacked the gold ore area at the old abandoned mines of the Paranapanema Company in order to capture resources to be used in their subversive actions.

The above incidents demonstrated a new threat to Brazilian sovereignty: an alliance among narco-traffickers, guerrillas and illegal miners. In essence, the current problems existing in the Amazon involve the Indian difficulties, clandestine mining and the smuggling of precious minerals that can be linked to foreign guerrillas and drug traffickers. In addition, the geographic characteristics of the Amazon, the precarious living standards of its occupants and the environmental and agrarian issues combine to present threats to the vital interests of Brazil in the Amazon. These problems specifically concern territorial integrity and national sovereignty.

GOVERNMENTAL ACTIONS FOR IMPLEMENTING THE DEFENSE POLICY

PRESIDENTIAL LEADERSHIP

The international system of law and the special characteristics of the Brazilian state have influenced the establishment of defense policy and President Fernando Henrique Cardoso has played a leading role in implementing this policy.

President Cardoso is one of the most academically qualified presidents in the long history of Brazil. A brilliant intellectual, he is a world-renowned sociologist and author of more that 100 monographs, including two dozen books, many of them written in English. In addition to Portuguese, he speaks English, French, Spanish and several other foreign languages. For most of his life, he was a university professor and taught at the University of São Paulo until 1964. He was in Santiago, Chile, from 1964 to 1968 and during this period he co-authored, with the Chilean sociologist Enzo Faletto, "Dependency and Development in Latin America" considered to be one of the most influential interpretations of twentieth-century Latin American structural dynamics. It attributes Latin America's slow development to the region's dependence on foreign capital and technology.[21] This thesis has been superseded by the concepts of free enterprise economics and regional integration.

President Cardoso also taught in France at the University of Paris (The Sorbonne), at Oxford University in Britain, and in the United States at the University of California (Berkeley), Princeton, Stanford and Yale. In the 1970's he became the best-known critic of the Brazilian nationalistic development model which was based on the strategy of state-led import-substitution industrialization. By the late 1970's, President Cardoso returned to São Paulo. He entered politics in 1977 and in 1983 he was elected as a national Senator. He was re-elected in 1986. During the period 1983-1992 he actively worked in several special committees of the Senate (Education, Justice and Citizenship, Foreign Relations and Economic Affairs). In June 1988 he helped to found the Brazilian Social Democracy Party (PSDB), a Center Left Party. President Cardoso was in Itamar Franco's Cabinet as the Minister of Foreign Relations. In May 1993, he moved to the Ministry of Finance as Minister, where he launched the "Real Plan for Economic Stabilization" in March 1994.[22] In November 1994 he was elected President and four years later he was reelected.

The President is deeply knowledgeable of Brazilian internal problems and very conscious of Brazil's image abroad as well as its relations with the international community. His experience and training make him uniquely qualified to lead the nation in solving the many problems Brazil faces in the country and on the international stage. The first priority in his government was to promote reform of key sections of the 1988 constitution primary in order to reduce the rule of the state in the economy and reform the federal bureaucracy.

Although defense issues had not received high priority in this program of government, within the context of constitutional reform, he has created the Ministry of Defense[23] that provokes deep changes in the structure of military power. Moreover, his program to conduct the foreign policy as well as social and economic policy has reflected in the defense arena.

DIPLOMACY

Regional Integration

The defense policy has given high value to diplomatic actions as the first tools to resolve disputes. Force may be used only for self-defense. In consequence, Brazilian diplomacy has been working to build friendly and cooperative relationships with the neighboring countries and partners in others continents. It aims to integrate Brazil both in the regional and global system.

In the regional context, in the past few years, Brazil has initiated a process of multilateral relations in the Amazon Basin and Southern Cone, represented in the Amazon Pact[24] and by the Common Market of South (Mercosul).[25] It has deepened and solidified the ties of friendship and cooperation between the nations located in the mentioned areas. The increasing consolidation of these integration processes not only has provided more specific weight for member nations in the international system, but also has contributed to reduce ongoing conflicts.

Thanks to the integration process in the Southern Cone provided by Mercosul, the Brazilian Armed Forces unilaterally abandoned the concept that Brazil and Argentine were strategic enemies. As one result, Brazil has moved two brigades from the southern region to the Amazon area. Nowadays, Brazil maintains in the southern boundaries, only a force enough to keep the balance of power with our neighbors.[26]

Brazil, Bolivia, Colombia, Ecuador, Guyana, Peru, Suriname and Venezuela have established the Amazon Pact[27] that aims to promote harmonious development of Amazon in order to raise the living standard of its population and integrate them in their respective national territories and economies. The pact also point out that social economic development and environmental preservation are responsibilities of each State and that cooperation among the member will help each other accomplish these responsibilities. In other words, It suggests the integration and solidarity as a way to resolve common problems.

Military-Military Relationship

The Armed Forces have been supporting this foreign policy by establishing military-military relations in the Amazon.

In 1998, the Brazilian Navy, took part in joint exercises with the Venezuelan Navy, as well as operational visits in South American and Caribbean ports. It also has implemented exchange programs related to operations, science and technology, instructions and logistics, which involve Bolivia, Colombia, Ecuador, Guyana and Venezuela.

10

The Brazilian Army has actively participated in the Conference of American Armies as well as has promoted symposiums and other activities with armies of neighboring countries. In September of 1998, the Brazilian Army sponsored a meeting of Amazon-country armies. The event had as its objective the exchange of opinions about common interests and the strengthening measures of respect, confidence and security for the Amazon. In September of 1998, Brazil and Venezuela signed an agreement for military cooperation.[29]

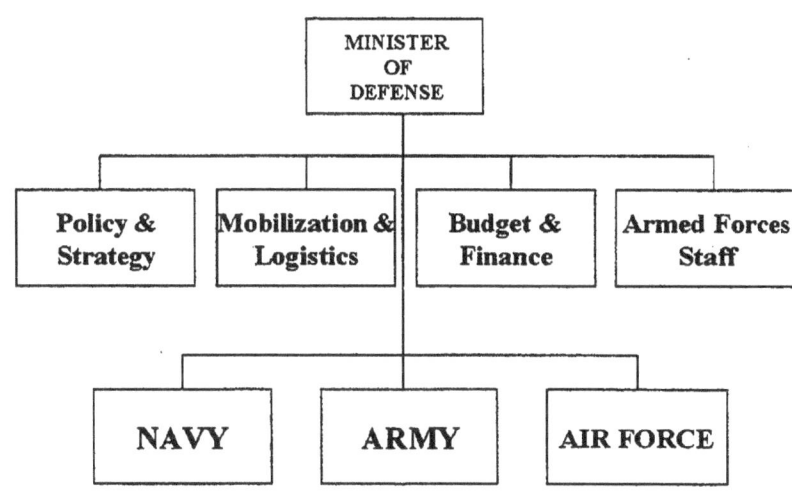

FIGURE 4 - MINISTER OF DEFENSE[28]

International System

In the global context, Brazil has reinforced its contribution to strengthen international peace and security by working actively to consolidate a multilateral regime that aims at global disarmament through the dismantling of stockpiles of nuclear weapons and others weapons of mass destruction. The country has signed international mechanism such as Non-proliferation Treaty, Missile Treaty Control Regime, Treaty of Tlateloco and the Convention for the elimination of chemical weapons.[30]

However, there is growing concern about the impact that Amazon problems have been causing in the international community as well with diplomatic novelties that distort "noble causes" and "new ideas".

With the end the Cold War the international law has been evolving. For instance, look at "noble causes" like human rights, rights of minorities, social justice and indigenous people or "new ideas" like limited sovereignty, the duty to interfere, the right to intervene, and humanitarian intervention. Who knows are used? For these reasons Brazilian diplomacy seeks to participate increasingly in the significant international decision-making processes, particularly in the United Nations and its Security Council. In short, Brazilian diplomacy will be oriented towards working to shape a ring of peace around the country and give Brazil a significant role in international affairs.[31]

MILITARY POWER

Ministry of Defense

In the last decades, there was a ministry for each of the armed force in the Brazilian government. The Army, Navy and Air Force had autonomy to establish their own priorities. To coordinate the activities among the military ministries there was the Armed Forces General Staff linked directly in the Presidency of the Republic. Strategic projects and programs were coordinated by Secretariat for Strategic Affairs that was also linked directly to the Presidency of the Republic.

In July 1999, the President of the Republic created the Ministry of Defense and simultaneously abolished the military ministries, the Armed Forces General Staff and the Secretariat for Strategic Affairs. The Army, the Navy and the Air Force ministries and the Armed Forces General Staff were integrated into the new ministry as subordinate commands while the Strategic Projects and Programs related to national security became part of its responsibilities. The Ministry of Defense is responsible for implementing the National Defense Policy.[32] While it is preparing the Brazilian Military Strategy to orient the actions of the armed forces, each of the services is continuing to develop their respective strategies. Likewise the strategic projects and programs are in process.

The Armed Forces

The armed forces missions are accomplished by the development of three types of activities: end activities, mid-activities and subsidiary activities.

The end activities are related to the operational use of the forces in armed conflict and in preparations related to the same. The mid-activities include the forces' support activities basically relate to administrative activities and the manner in which they are distributed throughout the national territory. The subsidiary activities include the social and economic areas and address the construction of the infra-structure of transportation, colonization, education, health, support to the civilian population in needy areas, support during public calamities and in several other areas which involve emergency situations.

In this context, the Brazilian Navy has a fleet in the region, with important bases in Belém and Manaus. It patrols the Amazon and provides a communications link throughout the Amazon Basin, maintaining a constant presence in practically all of the Basin's rivers. Another important unit of the Brazilian Navy, in the Amazon, is the Marine Force. Soldiers of this elite unit are trained in jungle warfare tactics, landing operations, commando attacks and boarding of vessels of all sizes.

As, subsidiary activities, humanitarian missions are conducted by two hospital ships - the Oswaldo Cruz and the Carlos Chagas - which are fundamental in providing health support to the riverine populations. Moreover, The Navy has been supporting practically all the social programs of the Federal and State Governments and municipalities.

The Brazilian Air Force (FAB) is a fundamental factor in taming, integrating and maintaining a presence in the Amazon. In spite of unfavorable conditions of air space and land in inaccessible region , FAB can act as a rapid response force. At present, FAB concentrates its training in the region, accomplishing real missions of supplying several small Army units spread throughout the area as well as whatever medical air evacuations become necessary.

The difficulties in navigating the Amazon rivers during the dry season causes the isolation of some of the Army border units as well as of communities that are near military compounds. They depend on, almost exclusively, FAB planes for their survival. Fighter aircraft are highly capable of acting efficiently in the Amazon, to protect air space sovereignty in the region. The FAB has been accomplishing missions of elevated social reach in remote Indian population areas as well as those of religious missions, border platoons, isolated towns and also special projects within inside the jungle. Today the airplane is still the only means to reach many of the areas of the Amazon. In addition, the technological knowledge and participation of engineers in the Air Force in building ever longer and better quality runways in the remote reaches of the jungle has allowed even C-130 aircraft to land in these remote northern area.

The Brazilian Army has been targeted this immense area as a strategic priority and is transferring military units from other areas of country into the Amazon. The Land Force has structured itself to enable employment highly specialized troops within the region. The Army keeps about 20,000 troops in the region under subordination of the Amazon Military Command (CMA) that is organized by 4 jungle infantry brigades, 2 logistic-administrative commands, 1 Construction Engineer Command and several units linked directly.[33] Officers and sergeants are trained at the Center for Instruction of Jungle Warfare (CIGS) and the rest of the troops acquire their training at several jungles units that make up the Amazon Military Command.

In the health field area, the Army has always provided medical and hospital assistance to civilian populations and Indian communities of the Amazon in several areas, where their nurses and doctors are, oftentimes, the only professionals present. In twenty-nine localities, exclusively Army health professionals provide medical assistance. In Tabatinga, for example, at the border with Colombia and Peru, the Garrison Hospital registers a daily average of 250 cases, counting on a potential clientele of approximately 40.000 patients, of which 95% are civilian. In São Gabriel da Cachoeira, in the state of the Amazon, the Military Hospital takes care of a civilian community of nearly 31.000 people.[34]

As part of this effort to improve the level of health care in country areas and at the nation's borders, the signing of an agreement of technical cooperation between the Ministers of Communications and the Army occurred in October of 1994, for the purpose of establishing two systems of tele-medicine. These systems already enable simultaneous medical discussions between professional miles apart thus allowing for faster diagnosis with more precision, safety and speed.

Although the Brazilian Army is not responsible for Indian issues, it is concerned with the indigenous populations and with the preservation of their reservations. Its participation consists of supporting the fight against illegal mining in Indian territory, developed by units of the Brazilian Army.

Army engineering has its presence in the region marked by construction, and conservation and repair of roads and other works of imperative importance to life in the Amazon. Relevant also is their work in cartography and mapping, demarcation of Indian reservations and environmentally protected areas and, more recently, rural colonization on land donated by the Army for agrarian reform.

In the war against drugs, the armed forces take part by accomplishing their constitutional missions of protecting and surveilling land boundaries, air space, seacoast and rivers as well as supervising the trade of armaments. They also have been providing logistical and intelligence support to the Federal

Police that is responsible for pursuing the drug war. In the same manner, the Army has trained members of the Special Battalion of Military Police.

Strategic Programs and Projects.

With the abolishment of Secretariat for Strategic Affairs, the functions of the System to Protect the Amazon / System for Surveillance of the Amazon Project, the Northern Bank Programs and Program of Financial Aid for Municipal Districts located on the boundaries were all transferred to the Ministry of Defense.

The Brazilian Government has been devoting a great deal of attention to the Amazon for the purpose of promoting a process of harmony between the social economic development and human and environmental needs. Regardless of the efforts by government, it has still has not been possible to reach the desired goals because of the shortage of means which would ensure efficient control over this immense area.

At the 1980's, activities considered damaging to national interests, such as predatory exploration, drug trafficking, damage to the environment and the wrongful use of Indian reservations have increasingly risen. Consequently, an urgent need has arisen to use adequate technological and trustworthy resources for the purpose of collecting, dealing with and routing information essential for allowing the government to transform it all into practical results and policy directives established for the Amazon.

Thus, on September 1990, the President of the Republic issued directives to create an effective national system that involves Ministry of Justice, Air Force Ministry and the Secretariat for Strategic Affairs. The Secretariat of Strategic Affairs was directed to develop and put into effect a National System of Coordination (today, SIPAM-System to Protect the Amazon). Its purpose was to integrate actions with other government agencies in the repression of illegal activities and in protecting the Amazon environment, underlining the responsibilities in this of the Brazilian Institute for the Environment and the Renewable Natural Resources agency-IBAMA. The Air Force Ministry must develop the System for Surveillance of the Amazon, (SIVAM) integrated to SIPAM. Finally, the Ministry of Justice must develop a package of measures, which will allow it to integrate the system, enabling it to implement actions for which it is responsible.

The mission of SIVAM[35] is, therefore, to collect, process, and produce and disclose data of interest to organizations, which make up SIPAM. Its areas of responsibility are:

- Environmental surveillance

- Aerial and surface surveillance

- Meteorological monitoring

- Communications monitoring

- Air traffic control and

- Planning and control of operations

The well-known Northern Bank program was created in 1985 to face challenges in the Amazon Region.

The geographic area of the program includes land in the states of the Amazon and Para, located on the left margin of the Solimões and Amazon rivers and includes, the states of Roraima and Amapa, a total are of approximately 1.221.000 km2. After extensive study, three different kinds of areas have been identified in Amazon:

- Border area between Tabatinga (AM) and Oiapoque (AP);

- The riverine margins of the rivers Solimões and Amazon and

- Interior nucleus.

The importance of the presence of the state in the area along the northern border to promote its development on equal terms with the initiative of neighboring countries was the factor that led this area to be recommended for the priority of immediate action.

The Northern Bank Program is established for some special projects such as:

- Increase of military presence in the area;

- More FUNAI (the National Indian Foundation) activity at the border area;

- Intensifying of campaigns to recover border markers;

- Improvement the transportation infra-structure; and

- Increase the offering of basic social resources.

The Special Project to Increase the Military Presence in the Amazon has the purpose of strengthening the Military expression of national power. Besides, It establishes that the armed forces, by the capillary-like peculiarity of their organization and distribution, must contribute to the livelihood of the border area and its development. This contribution would be done by supporting federal and state bureaus by implementing government action, particularly within the areas of education, health, transportation and telecommunications.

As a consequence of this project, the armed forces have developed the following initiatives and measures.[36]

- Construction of small hydroelectric power plants, health units, centers for food distribution, landing strips and military units at the borders;

- Assistance to Indian communities;

- Implementation of specific agriculture and livestock projects and telecommunications centers;

- Development of projects to increase water, land and air surveillance;

- Impounding, treatment and distribution of water;

- Expansion and improvement of hospitals;

- Mobile medical and dental support services; and

- Demarcation of the border, with more than sixty markers.

The Program of Financial Aid to the municipal districts located in the border was created in 1955 and revitalized in the current government. The program aim to assure some Brazilian state presence in the most remote areas of the country, helping those population to obtain some development and improvements in its well-being. It also seeks to take part of national effort to reduce the rural exodus and migration for the largest urban center as well as to contribute for neutralization of illicit activities on the border, through the creation of job alternatives and to strengthen the municipal structure.

In 1997 and 1998, the program accomplished a total of 656 projects at the border places. Among them, were built 32 schools and 39 health centers, other 61 school and 29 health centers were reformed. In order to improve the local infrastructure 68 bridges, sanitary units, day care were built and an airport modernized.[37]

ECONOMIC POWER

National Integrated Policy for Legal Amazon

At present, there are over 150 projects that benefit the riverine population, indigenous communities and small farmers who depend on extractive activities. There are also projects related to science and research towards Amazon future progress. In 1995, the Government issued the National Integrated Policy for the Legal Amazon that aims to arise the living standards of the local populations, through sustainable economic growth, broad utilization of natural and cultural resources, and improvement of income distribution.[38] Today, the Amazon economy involves diversified activities that range from extractive activities to electronic industry. Three areas support the most important part of the productive structure: the Carajás Project, Belém-Barcarema Region and the Manaus Free Zone. Likewise important are the agricultural area and industry located on southeastern Pará, Tocantins, northern Mato Grosso, and Rondônia. On the other hand, recent experiences in the regions have resulted in new possibilities of using forest and water resources.

Therefore, the regional development model has been seeking a balanced distribution of economic activities and, use of natural resources as well as social benefits. As result, the ongoing projects had to be reappraised and a new orientation directed to productive structure has been conducted in order to:

- renew, by using new technologies, economic activities that cause environmental and social impact, such as mining, lumber, agriculture, and others;

- modernize and reenergize traditional activities such as fishing, extractive activities, agriculture and fluvial navigation;

- develop and implement new activities that have great economic potential and environmental sustainability; and

- provide adequate infrastructure to the urban nucleus.[39]

In April 1997, at the opening ceremony of the Madeira-Amazonas Waterway, the President expressed how he intended to implement this policy:

"The Amazon population needs energy, transportation, agricultural production, jobs and prosperity."[40]

Brazil in Action Program

In this context, the Program "Brazil in Action" consists of 42 priority development projects and activities valued almost at R$ 79 billion. They are designed to ensure the physical and human infrastructure needed to promote investment. These projects were selected on the basis of their potential to stimulate productive investment and growth.[41]

In the Amazon this program has prioritized: the paving of highway BR-174 from Manaus to the boundary with Venezuela; improvement of conditions of highway BR-364/163; construction of the waterways Madeira-Amazonas and Araguaia-Tocantins; construction of a pipeline for the natural gas of Urucu, and transmission lines from Tucuruí hydroelectric.

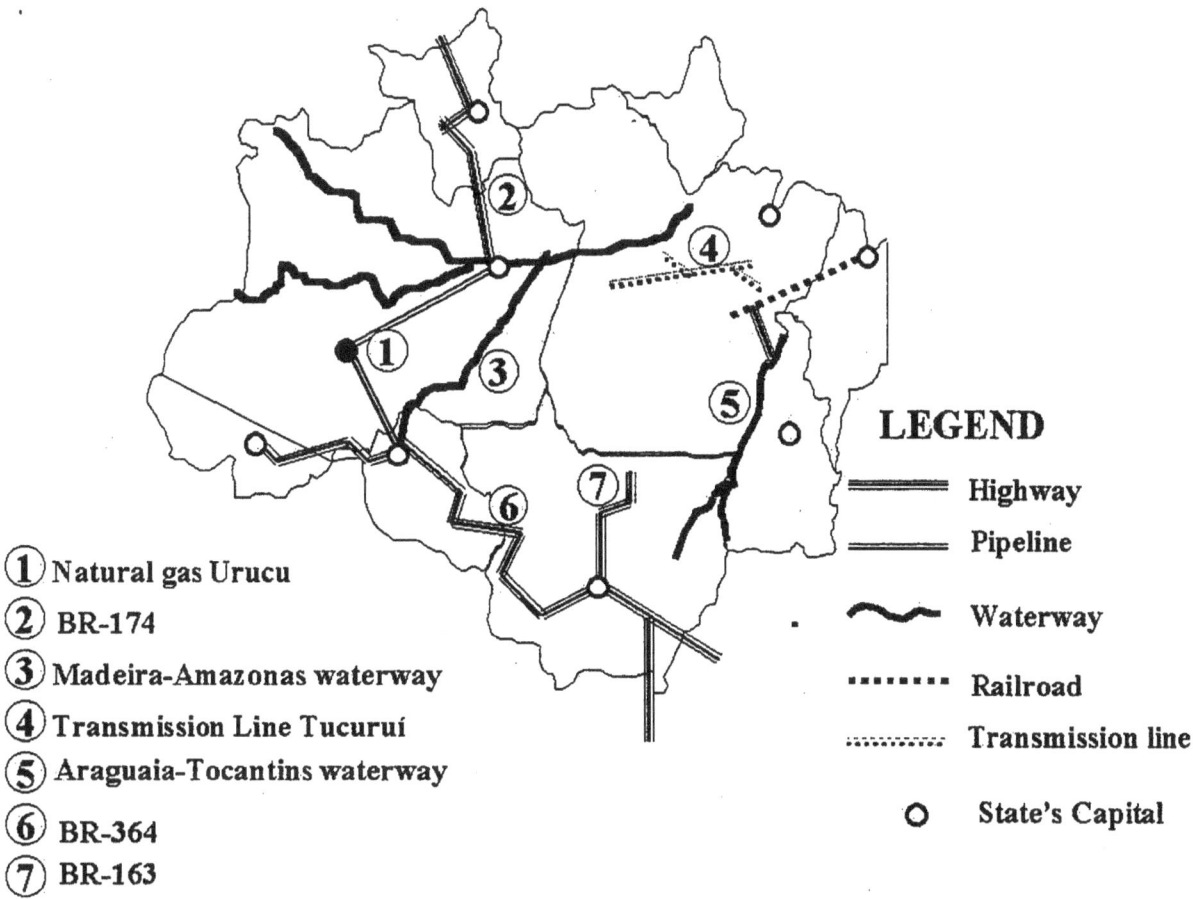

① Natural gas Urucu
② BR-174
③ Madeira-Amazonas waterway
④ Transmission Line Tucuruí
⑤ Araguaia-Tocantins waterway
⑥ BR-364
⑦ BR-163

LEGEND
═══ Highway
─── Pipeline
〰 Waterway
▪▪▪▪▪▪▪▪ Railroad
··········· Transmission line
O State's Capital

FIGURE 5 - BRAZIL IN ACTION PROGRAM[42]

After paving highway BR-174, an area over six million hectares became available for agriculture. In consequence, the National Bank for Economic and Social Development (BNDES) is preparing a multi-sector program to create a new agricultural frontier by promoting rational and organized occupation of this area. The program includes improvement of infrastructure such as roads and warehousing, establishment of agricultural industries and measures for environmental protection. Moreover, the Brazilian Enterprise

17

for Agricultural Research must study the local soil condition and suggest the most adequate products for the region. The BNDES will provide credit for small and medium farmers who wish to move into the new agricultural frontier. The National Institute for Settlement and Agrarian Reform may buy land in the region to settle landless workers.[43]

The improvement of conditions of highway BR-364/163 will reduce about 1700 km, the transportation distance between the productive region in the states of Acre, Rondonia and Mato Grosso to export harbors. The production that used to go to the southeast region, can today take the BR-364/163 up to the Madeira-Amazonas Waterway to reach the ports of Manaus and Belém, and from there be exported to other countries throughout the world.

The Madeira-Amazonas Waterway has been operating since April 1997. The Madeira River is available for navigation all year, even during the night, along a length 1056-km from Porto Velho-RO, to Itacoatiara, on the Amazon River near Manaus.[44]

Another important waterway is the Araguaia-Tocantins that consists of establishing a mixed corridor of transportation linking the Central region of the country with Itaqui Port in São Luiz, Maranhão. It is integrated with the highway BR-153, in the state of Pará, and the railroad North-South, in the state of Maranhão.

The Natural Gas Project of Urucu consists of transporting natural gas from Urucu located in the Amazon Basin to Manaus (Amazonas) and Porto Velho (Rondônia), over a distance of 700km; adapting the existent thermoelectric and building 500 km of transmission lines between Porto Velho and Rio Branco (Acre). To supply western Pará, there is a project underway to build a transmission line of 1007 km, from the Tucuruí Hydroelectric plant to the region.[45]

While the Brazil in Action Program is providing the improvement in the infrastructure, the Brazilian National Program for Agrarian Reform aims to create productive and profitable employment for Brazilians who seek their livelihoods in the countryside by increasing agricultural activities.

National Program for Agrarian Reform

As mentioned earlier, the Amazon presents a number of agrarian conflicts that involve different actors. There are taking place project to expanding the Brazilian agricultural frontier. Therefore, the government's problem is not just providing lands for distribution. It is necessary that various ministries and public institutions promote the survival of the settlements needed to guarantee specific programs and measures: subsidized credits for agriculture and for the construction of homes, roads, warehouses, schools, and health centers; family nutrition and the creation of cooperatives; etc. In other words, the great challenge of agrarian reform today is guaranteeing the economic viability of the settlements. For these reasons, the government has created such as the Special Credit Program for Agrarian Reform, (PROCERA), the Threshold (Lumiar) Project, the National Program to Strengthen Family Farming Program for the Support of the Development of Amazon and others.

PROCERA is the government's principal program. It guarantees subsidized resources, half of which the settler will not have to repay to the government. These resources are for financing the entire productive process: working expenses, investments, and payment of the settler's quota to the cooperative to which he belongs. However, these resources do not finance establishment of the economic and social infrastructure of the settlements, which is the responsibility of the government.[46]

The Threshold (Lumiar) Project, in its initial phase of implementation, provides a decentralized technical support service for the families of farmers resettled by the agrarian reform program. This is an initiative of the federal government, through the Special Ministry for Landed Property Policy. The project involves other federal agencies, banks, entities representative of the rural workers; and a representation of the state governments, preferably the secretary of agriculture.[47]

The project authorizes the formation of local technical assistance and professional training teams to guide the autonomous development of the settlers. For each group of 300 families, there will be one permanent local team, comprised of four professionals, two with university degrees (one specializing in farming, the other in administrative support and community organization) and two technicians. The program's objective is to empower the settlers, through a collective apprenticeship process, to make their settlements autonomous as soon as possible.

The National Program to Strengthen Family Farming was created during the current administration. It is subordinated to the Ministry of Agriculture and Food Supply. The Program provides credit at favorable interest rates to small family farmers - owners, squatters, renters or sharecroppers - and to production cooperatives and associations as long as they are formed by small producers. The borrowers can use these resources to cover harvest and farming expenses or to invest in machinery, equipment, new or used production goods, and other indispensable infrastructure items.[48]

The money can be used for investment projects, current expenses or working capital, either directly or as advances to cooperative members. The agrarian reform program not only has created programs at the national level but also has created specific programs to the Amazon region in order to assist the population that live in the rain forest.

The opening of the domestic Brazilian market threatens to end a principal income source of Amazon traditional populations - native rubber extraction. Rubber imported from Southeast Asia sells in Brazil for US$1.60 per kilo, while domestic rubber costs US$2.60. Custodians of the forest, the rubber gatherers and other small extractors are abandoning the woods and going to the cities in order to survive. If these traditional Amazon populations leave the forest, illegal woodcutters, domestic and foreign, will enter more easily, felling trees and selling the highly valued lumber.

In March 1997, the government decided that it would be the guarantor of the traditional forest populations. It gave them access to a special line of credit valued at R$24 million, of the Program for the Support of the Development of Amazon in order to contain the region's rural exodus and to preserve the forest resources. This program was created in 1996. It directs its resources to the 80,000 families in Amazon that earn their livelihoods from extractive activities, processing and selling products such as rubber, cashews, babassu, cabbage-palm and fish. In addition to resources for investments, the workers of the Amazon will have money for food and housing.

Less for economic reasons than for environmental security, the government will impede the collapse caused by imported rubber by making up the price differential between domestic and Asian rubber. Today, Brazil produces 4,000 tons of rubber annually and the rubber extractors' compensation will be approximately R$4 million annually.[49] The resources will come from Special Credit Program for Agrarian Reform and from National Program to Strengthen Family Farming.

Still in March of 1997, the government created the 450,000-hectares Extractive Reserve of Médio Juruá - the first in the state of Amazon. Its objective is to maintain the Amazon rainforest and the rubber gatherers within it, containing the devastation inflicted by the lumber companies and other predators. Combined with last year's legislation that increased from 50% to 80% the amount of forest to be preserved, obligatorily, on each rural property in northern Amazon, the foregoing measures constitutes the beginning of a true ecological agrarian reform for the Amazon region.

Another activity that can be supported by the Agrarian Reform Program is ecotourism. Ecotourism in the Amazon is an older phenomenon. The Amazon has been part of the international ecotourism circuit for years. It has grown and become sophisticated as it responds to the requirements of the tourists with the most purchasing power. Tourist activities in the rainforest have added more and better employment and income opportunities for the people who live along the River. Ecological tourism is contributing to efforts to reduce the exodus from the region, to preserve the environment and, at the same time, to guarantee a good financial return.

The outlook is for a rapid expansion of those activities, which have great economic potential for the region and do not threaten the equilibrium of the ecosystem. There is the expectation that rural properties will try to undertake ecotourism development programs.

Other measures

In the science and technology arena, the Brazilian Molecular Ecological Program for sustainable Use of Biodiversity (PROBAM) has just begun to build the Amazon Center of Biotechnology. There will be 26 research laboratories. The PROBAM aims to make possible the scientific research of Amazon biodiversity as well as to assure the intellectual property rights of regional natural wealth. The program is coordinated by Bioamazônia, an institution composed of 40% governmental participation and 60% of the private sector (most of them are university laboratories and research institutions).

In the form of international support, the Pilot Program to Conserve the Brazilian Rain Forest is investing $ 250 million to protect the forest and to promote sustainable development. It is a joint undertaking of the Brazilian Government, Brazil's civil society and the Group of seven (G-7) industrial countries.

As noticed in the foregoing, the Brazilian National Integrated Policy for Legal Amazon represents one sign of change in public policy for the area. By this way, the state act as coordinator and regulator, while numerous other entities participate in the development process.

CONCLUSION

In the final analysis, the Amazon is a strategic area where Brazil has vital interests. The ongoing problems in the region threaten particularly the national sovereignty and the territorial integrity. Although most directives established by the Brazilian National Defense Policy demand actions related with the Amazon, one of them is specific and determines:

"To protect the Brazilian Amazon, with the support of all Brazilian society and with high value given to the military presence."[50]

The military presence in the Amazon began in the early of XVII century, when the Portuguese started consolidating their possessions. The Army particularly has been increasing its presence by installing units in the boundary. Such units represent a focus of development that facilitate growth of new urban nuclei, granting Brazilian presence and sovereignty. This is a program of occupation and integration of that immense demographic empty area, by transferring military units from other parts of the country.

The establishment of Ministry of Defense will, in a further development of Brazilian military strategy, facilitate increasing presence in the area by all elements of the Armed Forces. It has become evident that full participation in the process by all segments of Brazilian society will permit social and economic development and will form the first line of national defense and the sustainability of the nation's sovereignty.

The combined implementation of both Defense Policy and an integrated policy for the Legal Amazon is the first step in designing a strategy for defending the area. In this process, the military contributions to the nation's development, as well as its response in emergency situations, remains a permanent part of the concept of military functions. It extends the national presence in the most remote parts of the country, guaranteeing safety and prosperity for the inhabitants and assuring them that they are a vital part of their nation's present and future.

In the past few years the largest issue concerning the Amazon was to decide between preserving or occupying the area. Experience proves the need to occupy the Amazon in order to preserve it. This approach has changed the focus of government action in the region.

In the international context, Brazilian diplomacy has been playing an important role in shaping a safe and peaceful environment. Furthermore, it demonstrates to the international community that the Brazilian people know what the Amazon means to mankind. In consequence, the world may lay to rest any concern about the Amazon, because Brazilian interest coincides with their interests.

Although the end objectives of Amazon controversies seems equitable, to preserve the Brazilian Amazon rain forest against destruction of its ecosystem as well as to defend the rights of all Brazilians who live in the region is the sole duty and responsibility of the Brazilian Government. International cooperation with Amazon sustainable development will be welcome but Brazil will not accept and will challenge any interference with its sovereign right.

The concretion of national defense objectives requires implementing a sustainable defense policy, toward the gradual modernization of self-defense capability. It depends on constructing a development model that strengthens democracy, reduces social inequality and regional imbalance. This model has to attend to political, social, economic and military priorities and be compatible with defense and diplomatic actions. Although the struggle has been long and difficult, with the dedication of major resources and the will to persevere, victory in this Amazon battle is assured.

Word count: 9,098 words

ENDNOTES

[1] U.S. National Defense University, <u>Strategic Assessment 1998 - Engaging Power for Peace</u>, (Fort Lesley J. McNair , Washington D.C.: Institute for National Strategic Studies, March 1998), 106.

[2] Ibid., 114.

[3] Rex A Hudson, <u>Brazil: a Country Study</u>. Area handbook series, 5th edition (Washington D.C: Federal Research Division - Library of Congress, 1998), 91

[4] Edmundo S. Fujita, "Uma Política de Defesa Sustentável para o Brasil". <u>Parcerias Estratégicas</u>, number 5 (September 1998), 106.

[5] Fernando Henrique Cardoso, Política de Defesa Nacional Brasileira (Brasília - DF: Presidência da República, November 1996), 8

[6] Ibid.,7.

[7] Amazon Surveillance System, available from http://www.sivam.gov.br/sivaning/amazonia/apres1.htm ; Internet, accessed 6 October 1999.

[8] Maria Helena Simielli, <u>Geoatlas</u> (São Paulo, SP: Ática S.A, 1995), 112.

[9] Amazon Surveillance System, available from http://www.sivam.gov.br/sivaning/amazonia/numerous1.htm ; Internet, accessed 6 October 1999.

[10] Water: the gold of the next millennium, available from http://www.sivam.gov.br/sivaning/amazonia/rigu2.htm , Internet, accessed 6 October 1999.

[11] Centro de Comunicação Social do Exército, "Amazônia: Vida, Combate e Trabalho", Produtos CCOMSEx - Fita 2, 1998. Videocassete.

[12] Preston E. James and C.W. Minkel, <u>Latin America</u> (New York, NY: John Wiley &Son 1985), 519.

[13] Ibid., 521

[14] Fernando Henrique Cardoso, <u>Reforma Agrária Compromisso de Todos</u> (Brasília - DF: Presidência da República, 1997), 41.

[15] Álvaro Pinheiro de Souza and Willian Mendell, <u>Guerrilla in the Brazilian Amazon</u> (Fort Leavenworth, Kansas: Foreign Military Studies Office, July 1995), 5.

[16] Rex A., LXXVI

[17] "Amazônia" linked from Exército Brasileiro at "Produtos Especiais" available from http://www.exercito.gov.br/exebra/indio/indios.htm. Internet, accessed 8 October 1999.

[18] Fernando Henrique Cardoso, <u>Sociedades Indígenas e a Ação do Governo</u> (Brasília - DF: Presidência da República, 1996), 6.

[19] Rex A., 372

[20] Álvaro, 12.

[21] Rex A., LXXVI

[22] "Biografia do Presidente", linked from Presidência da Republica Federativa do Brasil, available from http://www.planalto.gov.br/homepres/fhc-port.htm , Internet, accessed 4 March 2000.

[23] "Emenda Constitucional Nr 23", linked from Presidência da República Federativa do Brasil, available from http://www.planalto.gov.br/CCIVIL/constituição/emendas/emc/quadro_emc.htm, Internet, accessed 5 March 2000.

[24] "Tratado de Cooperação Amazônica", available from http://www.mre.gov.br/cdbrasil/itamaraty/web/port/relext/mre/orgreg/tcoopam/apresent.htm ; Internet accessed 4 March 2000.

[25] "Mercosul", available from http://www.mre.gov.br/cdbrasil/itamaraty/web/port/relext/mre/orgreg/mercom/apresent.htm ; Internet accessed 4 March 2000.

[26] Eliezer Risso de Oliveira,, "Política de defesa e Mercosul", 26 October 1997. Available from <http://www.unicamp.br/nee/PolDefMercosul.html>. Internet, accessed 8 October 1999.

[27] "Tratado de Cooperação Amazônica", available.from http://www.amazonia.exercito.gov.br/tratados/tratado.htm . Internet, accessed 8 October 1999.

[28] Gilberto Rodrigues Pimentel, "O Exército Brasileiro", briefing slides, Brazilian General Staff, Brazilian Army Head Quarter. Brasília - DF, 4 November 1999.

[29] "Mensagem ao Congresso Nacional 1999 - Relações Internacionais", linked from Presidência da República Federativa do Brasil, available from http://www.planalto.gov.br/secom/coleção/99mens8.htm. Internet, accessed 8 October 1999.

[30] Ibid.

[31] Fernando, Política de Defesa Nacional, 6.

[32] "Lei complementar Nr 97, linked from Presidência da República Federativa do Brasil, available from http://www.planalto.gov.br/CCIVIL/leis/LCP/quadro_lcp.htm. Internet, accessed 5 March 2000.

[33] "Amazônia" linked from Exército Brasileiro at "Produtos Especiais" available from http://www.exercito.gov.br . Internet, accessed 8 october 1999.

[34] Presidência da República, Estado-Maior das Forças Armadas. O Brasil e suas Forças Armadas (Brasília - DF 1996),35.

[35] Ibid., 52.

[36] Ibid.,54.

[37] "Mensagem ao Congresso Nacional 1999 - Presença do Estado na faixa de fronteira" linked from Presidência da República Federativa do Brasil, available from http://www.planalto.gov.br/secom/coleção/99mens8.htm. Internet, accessed 8 October 1999.

[38] Ministério do Meio Ambiente, dos Recursos Hídricos a da Amazônia Legal, Secretaria de Coordenação dos Assuntos da Amazônia Legal. Política Integrada para Amazonia Legal (Brasília - DF, July 1995), 19.

[39] Ibid.,20.

[40] Fernando Henrique Cardoso, Trechos de Pronunciamentos do Presidente da República (Brasília - DF: Presidência da República, 1998), 21.

[41] Fernando, Programa Brasil em Ação - Dois anos (Brasília - DF: Presidência da República, 1998), 5.

[42] Fernando, Programa Brasil em Ação - Dois anos, 1.

[43] Fernando, Trechos de Pronunciamentos do Presidente da República, 24.

[44] Fernando, Programa Brasil em Ação - Dois anos, 52.

[45] Ibid.,65.

[46] Fernando, Reforma Agrária Compromisso de Todos, 31.

[47] Ibid., 32.

[48] Ibid., 60.

[49] Ibid., 70.

[50] Fernando, Política de Defesa Nacional, 10.

BIBLIOGRAPHY

Amazonia. Linked from Exército Brasileiro at "Produtos Especiais". Available from http://www.exercito.gov.br;. Internet, accessed 8 october 1999.

Biografia do Presidente. Linked from Presidência da República Federativa do Brasil, available from http://www.planalto.gov.br/homepres/fhc-port.htm , Internet, accessed 4 March 2000.

Cardoso, Fernando Henrique, "Discurso sobre a Política de Defesa Nacional." Parcerias Estratégicas, Volume 1, number 1, December 1996, 16-18.

_____ Trechos de Pronunciamentos do Presidente da República. Brasília - DF: Presidência da República, 1998.

_____. Brazilian National Defense Policy. Brasília - DF: Presidência da República, 1998.

_____. O Brasil e suas Forças Armadas. Brasília - DF: Presidência da República, Estado-Maior das Forças Armadas, 1996.

_____. Política Integrada para Amazonia legal .Brasília - DF: Ministério do Meio Ambiente, dos Recursos Hídricos a da Amazônia Legal, Secretaria de Coordenação ods Assuntos da Amazônia Legal, July 1995.

_____. Programa Brasil em Ação - Dois anos. Brasília - DF: Presidência da República, 1998.

_____. Reforma Agrária - Compromisso de Todos. Brasília - DF: Presidência da República, 1997.

_____. Sociedades Índígenas e Ação do Governo. Brasília - DF: Presidência da República, 1996.

Emenda Constitucional Nr 23.Linked from Presidência da República Federativa do Brasil, available from http://www.planalto.gov.br/CCIVIL/constituição/emendas/emc/quadro_emc.htm, Internet, accessed 5 March 2000.

Fujita, Edmundo S., "Uma Política de Defesa Sustentável para o Brasil." Parcerias Estratégicas, number 5 , September 1998, 101-112.

Hudson, Rex A., Brazil: a Country Study. Area handbook series, 5th edition. Washington D.C: Federal Research Division - Library of Congress, 1998.

James, Preston E., and C.W. Minkel, Latin America, 5th edition. New York, NY: John Wiley & Son, 1985.

Lampreia, Luiz Felipe, "O Brasil e o Mundo no SéculoXXI." Parcerias Estratégicas, Volume 1, number 1, December 1996, 38-54.

Lei complementar Nr 97. Llinked from Presidência da República Federativa do Brasil, available from http://www.planalto.gov.br/CCIVIL/leis/LCP/quadro_lcp.htm. Internet, accessed 5 March 2000.

Menezes, Delano Teixeira, "A necessidade de uma Política de Defesa." Parcerias Estratégicas, number . 5, September 1998, 113-121.

Mensagem ao Congresso Nacional 1999. Linked from Presidência da República Federativa do Brasil, available from http://www.planalto.gov.br/secom/coleção/99mens8.htm. Internet, accessed 8 October 1999.

Mercosul. Linked from Ministério das Relações Exteriores, available from http://www.mre.gov.br/cdbrasil/itamaraty/web/port/relext/mre/orgreg/mercom/apresent.htm ; Internet, accessed 4 March 2000.

Oliveira, Eliezer Risso de, "Política de Defesa e Mercosul", 26 October 1997. Available from <http://www.unicamp.br/nee/PolDefMercosul.html>, Internet, accessed 8 October 1999.

Pilot Program to Conserve the Brazilian Rain Forest. Available from http://www.worldbank.org/html/extdr/offrep/lac/ppg7/overview.htm. Internet, accessed 06 October 1999.

Pinheiro, Álvaro de Souza, and Willian W. Mendel, "Guerilla in the Brazilian Amazon." Foreign Military Studies Office, Fort Leavenworth, Kansas, July 1995.

Schneider, Ronald M., Brazil, Culture and Politics in a New Industrial Powerhouse. Boulder, CO: Westview Press, Inc., 1996.

Simielli, Maria Helena, Geoatlas. São Paulo, SP: Ática S.A, 1995.

Tratado de Cooperação Amazônica". Linked from Ministério das Relações Exteriores, available from http://www.mre.gov.br/cdbrasil/itamaraty/web/port/relext/mre/orgreg/tcoopam/apresent.htm ; Internet, accessed 4 March 2000.

"Water: the gold of the next millennium." Available from http://www.sivam.gov.br/sivaning/amazonia/riqu2.htm , Internet, accessed 6 October 1999.

www.ingramcontent.com/pod-product-compliance
Lightning Source LLC
Chambersburg PA
CBHW081138280526
45787CB00007B/3133

* 9 7 8 1 5 2 2 7 8 5 6 3 7 *